Riffs

Translations, imitations and
adaptations

Translations, imitations and adaptations

George Simmers

Illustrations by
Bruno Vars

Snakeskin 2023

This collection is published by:
Snakeskin,
9 Priestley Grove,
Huddersfield
HD4 7RG

Set in Palatino
Printed by Lulu

ISBN: 978-1-4467-6462-6

Thanks to the HWG Poetry Days, which stimulated many of these versions. In particular, thanks to Ken and Tim for Ovid and Virgil, and to Chris for the Greek Anthology.

Ovid

Once,

before earth was earth, or sea was sea,
Before there was a sky to canopy
Our world, when just inert accumulated
Matter existed, uncoordinated,
Randomly lacking meaning, shape or form,
There was no sun to brighten or to warm,
No sky existed, so no moon shone there,
Nor did our earth hang poised, enclosed by air.

There were no shores to be embraced by sea.
Though water there was, and land - disturbingly
They were the same; the solids then had no
Distinctive firmness; liquids did not flow.
Each thing was muddled with what it was not:
Soft sapped the hard, cold nullified the hot.
Moistness fought dryness, heaviness sapped the light.
Nothing could be itself, day merged itself with night.

But then some – what? some god perhaps? - some elevated
But natural force, at one stroke separated
Earth from the sky, made land distinct from sea,
Sorted the elements, and made them free
To be the the things they are, now difference
Can let them make their own harmonious sense.

Aether flies fierily to make the clear
And weightless sky, above the atmosphere,
While heavier earth sinks downward to its place,
Where it's held constant by the sea's embrace.

Above the world, the blazing stars now shone,
Bright gleaming fish lived in the sea, and on
The land roamed beasts, and in the yielding air
Flew all the birds whose proper place was there.

Yet of these creatures, none were on a par

With gods until Prometheus robbed a star,
Grabbed fire, mixed it with water and with earth,
Shaped it much like a god, and so gave birth
To man, a creature who can stand erect,
Lift up his head and stare at gods direct.
This was the way the human race began,
When earth was metamorphosed into man.

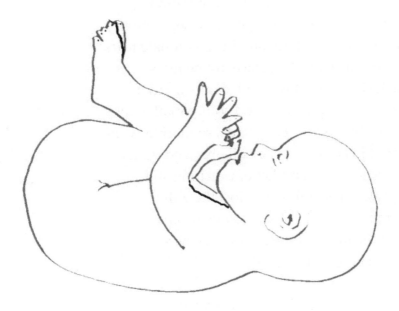

Narcissus

Without a thought for food or rest, he lies
Stretched out upon the shadowed grass, his eyes
Fixed on the watery mirror, and the sight
Undoes him, for he takes so fierce a joy
In what he sees, that lovely perfect boy.
He bends towards the face, which in return
Lifts up its lips to his, as though they yearn
With equal love.

        He feels in desperation
Death would be better now than separation.
Love overcomes him, and his passionate tears
Disturb the water's surface, till he fears
The losing of his love, and shouts in grief
'Oh can't my passions find some small relief
By touching you?' His hands, so marble-white
Beat at his naked breast, till, frenzied quite,
He cries 'Alas!', and Echo, watching still,
Repeats 'Alas!' for he has lost the will
To move at all, and motionless he lies
Until the night forever shuts the eyes
Whose image he adored.

        His life thus ended,
Narcissus, so the story goes, descended
To Hades and forever stares and weeps
Into his image in the Styx's deeps.

On earth his death was mourned by lovely Naiads,
Who savaged their hair in grief, and by the Dryads,
Whose wailings desperate Echo soon repeated.
His funeral pyre was raised, but not completed.
Narcissus' body could nowhere be found.
Instead, beside the river, on the ground
Where he had lain, a white and yellow flower
Bends to admire itself, hour after hour.

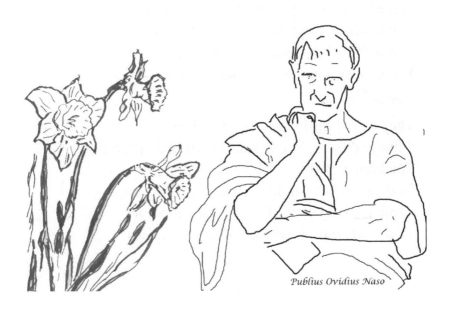

Publius Ovidius Naso

Orpheus sings in Hades

So Orpheus sang, and as his music swept
Through Hades, even bloodless shadows wept
To hear such music; even Tantalus paused
In his hard fruitless task. The magic caused
Ixion's wheel to stop; Prometheus' birds
Stopped snatching at his liver, as both words
And melody possessed them; by his rock
Sisyphus sat idle, in a trance of shock.
As struck as he, the doomed Dianides
Set down their urns, whilst fierce Eumenides
Wept actual tears; for once their sympathies
Were harrowed by mere human suffering.
Nor could Persephone nor Hades' king
Resist the song, could not deny the prayer
Whose lovely notes still lingered in the air.

They called Euridice, who from her place
Among the new-made shades, limped out to face
The loving husband who, heroically,
Had saved her. Mighty Hades made decree:
'Singer, she's yours. Together take the track
That leads out of Avernus. Don't look back.'

From **Ovid** *Metamorphoses*, **Book X**

Bacchus punishes the Bacchae

For Bacchus, dark fury at these mindless riots
And the savaging of Orpheus, whose melodies
Had made more precious still the precious rites
Of his own most secret, most sacred mysteries.
Bacchus struck the women fast. Hard roots

Zeroed down from their toe tips
To twist unmovable into solid ground.
Have you seen poor birds when they're caught in traps?
They struggle to be free, straining up into the wind,
But the fiercer they fight toward their tree-tops

The tighter they're clamped to unlovely ground.
It was like that. Roots pliable but unyielding
Were unmovable. And soon each woman found
The texture of ugly bark spreading
Upwards from toenails to toes, and around

Her ankles and creeping upward and up
To the curve of the calves, And when her hand
Moved down to prevent it, the thing would not stop,
But the slap of her hand on her thigh was the sound
Of oak on oak, and that bark would creep

Up over breasts and shoulders; inexorably
What had been human degenerated
To solid oak, Had you been there to see

Her jointed protesting arms, you would have stated
Those are branches of trees, definitely.

You'd have spoken with certainty
And would have been correct.
No sign remained of the woman wrecked,
Only a tree.

From
Metamorphoses,
Book X

Virgil

From **Aeneid Book VI**

Aeneas has met his his father, Anchises, in the underworld, among the dead. Anchises shows his son the marvels of the place, including a riverbank where the souls of the dead are crowding...

Anchises and his son then made
Their way through a green wooded glade
To where a quiet river roams
Meanderingly past peaceful homes.
Beneath a sky without a cloud,
Innumerable humans crowd,
Determined as the bees who swarm

About the blossom in the warm
And sensuous spring. Not knowing who
These people are, or what they do,
Aeneas asks his father: *What*
Could bring so many to this spot?

Anchises tells him: These, my son,
Are souls quite privileged; each one
Is owed a second life by fate,
A new chance in embodied state
To live again, but each must first
With Lethe water quench his thirst,
So gaining sweet forgetfulness
Of previous woes and life's duress.

But father, why should any man
Desire to leave this place, and can
He truly wish to live again
The human life of stress and pain?

Anchises told his doubting son:
Understand - all things are one.
The glorious sun, the moon and all
The stars and this our earthly ball;
Birds, fish and beasts of every kind
Are fragments of eternal mind.
There is a great and godly force
That fiercely runs its mighty course
Through earthly bodies born to die

Beneath the vast enveloping sky.
Poor humans, with their joys and tears,
Their bodily desires and fears,
Penned in the dungeon of the flesh
Can rarely glimpse how all things mesh.
They see but dimly heaven's light
While worldly burdens are their plight.
But when the last of life has fled,
And they see clearly, being dead,
They realise an earthly taint
Still keeps their beings in constraint.
They're still infected; then begins
A proper purging of their sins.
Some, exposed to air and sky,
The cleansing winds will purify;
Swirling floods and pelting rain
Will wash away another's stain;
Yet others need the heat of fire
To burn away impure desire.
It takes an age to shift the stain;
But some, the finest, will attain
Elisium, and these you see
Are souls who by divine decree
Are shepherded to Lethe's brink
And permitted then to drink
Forgetfulness, till with one taste
All memories will be effaced.
Forgetting human life is pain,
They are prepared to live again.

Interea videt Aeneas in valle reducta
seclusum nemus et virgulta sonantia silvae.
Lethaeumque domos placidas qui praenatat amnem.
hunc circum innumerae gentes populique volabant:
ac veluti in pratis ubi apes aestate serena
floribus insidunt variis et candida cir
lilia funduntur, strepit omnis mur
horrescit visu subito causasque requ
inscius Aeneas, quae sint ea flumir
quive viri tanto complerint agmine
tum pater Anchises: 'animae, quibus
corpora debentur, Lethaei ad fluminis
securos latices et longa oblivia potant.
has equidem memorare tibi atque ostender
iampridem, hanc prolem cupio enumera
quo magis Italia mecum laetere repe
'o pater, anne aliquas ad caelum hin
sublimis animas iterumque ad tarda
corpora? quae lucis miseris tam dira cupido?'
'dicam equidem nec te suspensum, nate, tenebo'

P. Vigilius Maro

Rumour

Through Africa vile Rumour raced,
Of all the plagues the fastest-paced.
She's supple, smart, light on her toes,
And gains momentum as she goes.
She may start small as creeping mouse
But soon she'll overtop the house
Till, though in muck her feet may stand,
Her head is in Cloud-Cuckoo-Land.
Watch Rumour go! Her huge black wings
Hide fearful eyes, a tongue that stings,
Lungs that can bellow till they burst
And ears fine-tuned to hear the worst.
By night she'll hiss round that odd place
Nor earth nor sky, but cyberspace,
And through those small hours she will keep
Alert and growing — she won't sleep.
Come daylight she'll observe with malice
Events in cottage and in palace.
Great cities then will shake in fear
At the enormities they hear,
And shudder when they taste the brew
In which she's mixed the false and true.
Whenever men, fraught with disgust,
All eye each other with mistrust,
Great Rumour grins, her strength unfurled.
She relishes our post-truth world!

from **Aeneid Book IV**

The Trojans enthusiastically bring the wooden horse into their City.

Now passionate, the crowd cries out: 'Ahead!
Into the City!' The huge horse is led
Lumbering city-wards. Now strong men broach
The walls to help the pregnant thing approach.
Wheels ease its progress; as with strong hemp ropes
It's dragged uphill. The City's future hopes
Inspire the joyful chants the children sing
Whose small hands thrill to touch the ropes that bring
This thing into the City. We observe with joy
Its hoisting up, and its smooth glide through Troy,
Our City, built by gods, made strong by war.
Four times its progress hit a halt, and four
Times a keen ear might hear within a clang
Like weaponry – yet still the great crowd sang
Encouragement; only Cassandra warned -
But she was just Cassandra, so was scorned.
She saw the City burning and laid waste,
But we ignored her ravings in wild haste
To celebrate, and deck our shrines with bay
And laurel, having no sense that the day
Might be the last we shared.

                The skies revolve
To bring the night whose shadows now dissolve
The active day. Our weary limbs sink deep
Into our beds for comfortable sleep.

                      From **Aeneid Book II**

Catullus

IV:

Look at it, friends: my bean-shaped boat
Was once the fastest thing afloat —
No question — nothing made of timber
With oars or sail-sheets was more limber.
Does the Adriatic coast deny it?
Did the Colossus when we sped by it?
No, nor did bleak and nasty Thrace —
And as for Cytorus, that's the place
Where long before she was a yacht
She existed, in some wooded spot
Upon a sunlit slope, a tree
Whose leaves kept moving, whisperingly.
Amastris, all of this you know,
And Cytorus, where box-trees grow
You watched her keenly when she first
Dipped in her oars and tried a burst
Of speed; you saw those oars that flashed
Through choppy seas, and how she dashed!
And whether winds blew East or West,

Or Jove gave calm, she, unimpressed,
Kept on. She never paused to make
Oblations just for safety's sake.
No, swift and surely see her go
To journey's end, to Sirmio.

But that was then; and this is now.
Today her once-so gallant prow
Rests far from the ocean's din,
An offering to Castor and his twin,
The pair who look protectively
On all who venture on the sea.

Sirmione

Gaius Valerius Catullus

VII

Lesbia, you ask me quantify
How many of your kisses I
Might think enough. My answer? Count,
When you're in Libya, the amount
Of tiny sand grains on the beach
Along the shining miles that reach
Between Jove's shrine and Battus's tomb.
Or count the stars that pierce the gloom
To stare all-seeing from above
Upon the privacies of love.
Let's kiss and kiss with such excess
We'll make all voyeurs' minds a mess;
Add kiss on kiss, till we've a sum
So vast all gossips are struck dumb.

XXXVIII

He's ailing, Cornificius; your Catullus is not well.
He's sinking by the minute and he's feverish as hell.
Yet you haven't come to visit; is that how friends behave
When a chum they've known for ages is careering to his
grave?
If you have any heart at all, you'll send a message, please,
Sopping with tragic empathy, like old Simonides.[1]

---

[1] Simonides (c. 556–468 BC) was a poet famous for the nobility of his epitaphs.

XLVI

So Spring is coming, to transform
Cold into warmth, and tame the storm
To amicable breezes. So,
Catullus, now's the time to go -
To turn your back on Phrygian fields,
And shun Bithynia, though it yields
Great riches. Now's the time to go
To famous cities I don't know,
Far-flung in Asia. Now my mind
Is all a-fidget, and I find
My feet refusing to keep still...

So farewell to my friends, who will
Like me be roaming far from Rome.
Each man must find his own way home.

CXIII

In Pompey's Consulate, Year One,
There were two of them, Cinna, sharing the fun
Of Lady Mucilla. In this second year,
Both still pursue the same career
But dozens of others have joined the game
And take their turn with that generous dame.
Which goes to show: adultery's seed
Shoots forth a most prolific weed.

The Greek Anthology

The Greek Anthology is a collection of epigrams written between the fifth century B.C. and the fifth century A.D.
The earliest epigrams were epitaphs. Later, poets wrote mock epitaphs, of which these four are a sample.

For the Tomb of the Poet Anacreon
by **Antipater of Sidon**
7.26
Stranger, here my bones are stored
And if my writing gave you pleasure
They'd be most grateful if you poured
A libation here, for wine I treasure
Above all else. I loved the rites
Of Bacchus, so benign, so royal,
Whose praise I'd sing on boozy nights,
Why should mere death make me disloyal?
Pour me some wine, that rich red wonder,
Even though I'm six feet under.

By **Crinagoras**

7.380

Tombs can mislead; this one is smooth and couth,
Its edges quite meticulously straight;
The mason's craft, however, hides the truth.
Don't judge him by his grave; it's deaf - can't hear
If he's still yammering lies beneath its weight.
Don't let this tombstone tempt you to a tear -
It's spiv Eunicides, whom none could trust
Who's here interred, and rotting into dust.

By **Damagetus**

7.497

Thymodes built this empty tomb, and wept
As he built it, for his son who has no grave
Here or elsewhere, but who at sea was swept
Away and lost beneath the grasping wave.
The father pictures bones washed up to bleach
Unmourned on some far distant lonely beach.

By **Julianus Aegyptus**

7:605

Rhodo, this stone urn and this marble tomb
Were here erected by your husband, whom
You pleased; and in addition he has paid
For prayers to be intoned to bless your shade.
He thus rewards your generosity
In dying early, which has set him free.

Three epigrams by Rufinus

Little is known about Rufinus except that he lived in either the fourth or fifth century A.D. Maybe. The fifth book of the Greek Anthology, which comprises amatory and erotic verses, is reckoned to be compiled by him, and includes many of his own epigrams.

5. 93

Eros I'll fight; my common sense
Should be an adequate defence.
Although he's an immortal, I
Shall look him soberly in the eye
And so withstand his cunning force.
Yes, I shall win –
                 unless, of course,
He teams with Bacchus. Two against one
Can't be resisted. I'm undone.

5.66

Prodike was alone. I made my pleas.
Undignified, I hugged her knees
And started to beseech and rave,
I told her none but she could save
A man half lost to mad despair.
Could I but hope that she might care...
A small tear glistened in her eye;
But carefully she wiped it dry
And, resisting my duress,
Said no, with infinite gentleness.

5.35

Three friendly ladies sought my aid in judging whose posterior
Might be definitively ranked aesthetically superior.
They quickly, quite forgetting any claims to be respectable,
Whipped off their lower garments so their backsides were
                                                    inspectable.
The first belongs to Rhodope, whose form is hardly willowy
Her bum is broad and bountiful, marshmallowy and pillowy.
The second is Melitis's; I think the most implacable
Of puritans would melt to see two cheeks so very smackable.
But now comes Rhodocleia, with a bum of tomboy slenderness
Inspiring any thinking heart to gentlemanly tenderness...

How could I judge? You will have read, perhaps in ancient
                                                    codices,
How Paris had to choose between three goddesses *sans* bodices.
Well, if to help my judging, I should call old Paris in, it is
A cert he'd much prefer my three to bums of mere divinities.

A poem by **Paulus Silentiarius**

(Or Paul the Usher). He was probably a civil servant in Byzantium in the sixth century A.D. In a Christian age, his poems reference the older gods. The *cithara* was more of a lyre than a guitar – but guitar seemed to fit the mood better.

6.54

Question: Why should Eunomus class
A grasshopper of polished brass
A fitting tribute to Apollo?
I'll explain – I trust you'll follow.

Eunomos, you'll have guessed, was Greek,
He was a star, a guitar-freak.
Every girl in Greece would thrill,
Just thinking of his fingering skill.
In him pure love of music raged,
And a festival found him engaged
With Parthis in a guitar quarrel
Whose prize would be the crown of laurel.
He played with joy; he caught a whiff
Of huge success; a final riff
Would end the gig triumphantly -
But – suddenly - catastrophe!
A string snapped with an ugly twang,
Threatening the whole shebang.
So were his chances all benighted?
No. A grasshopper alighted
On the stock of his guitar
And proved itself a music star

By offering a flattened G
Exactly where the melody
Demanded that the note should be.
Harmoniously, this was the goods,
And so the music of the woods
Chimed in with human melody
To make perfection, tunefully.
Together, human and cicada
Duetted with such style and ardour
The laurel crown was rightly theirs.

Eunomos modestly declares:
'Apollo's the cicada's lord,
It's he, not I, deserves reward.
That's why I keep that bronze grasshopper
In its place of honour, as is proper.'

Francois Villon

After killing a man in a fight, Francois Villon (1431-1463?) was condemned to be hanged. He was later reprieved, but this poem is his response to the experience.

Francois Villon

Epitaphe dudit Villon
Freres humains qui apres no9 biues
Nayez les cuers contre no9 endurcis
Car se pitie de no9 pouures auez
Dieu en aura pluftoft de bous mercis
Bous nous boies cy ataches cinq six
Quāt de la char q trop auōs nourrie
Elleft pieca deuouree et pourrie
et no9 les os deuendz cēdres a pouldre
De noftre mal personne ne sen rie
Mais pries-dieu que tous nous bueil
se absouldze   g iii.

Ballade of the Hanged Men

My fellow humans still among the living,
If you can look at us with hearts unhardened,
Can see us wretches, and can be forgiving,
Then trust in God that you too will be pardoned.
You see us strung up, five, six in a line,
With all that flesh we plumped with food and wine
Now pecked by birds or dried hard by the wind,
Until our disconnected bones drop off.
When you stare at our ugliness, don't scoff,
But pray to God to pardon all mankind.

If we call you brothers, please don't take offence.
Though justice wisely thinks us better dead.
You know enough to know that common sense
Can sometimes take its flight from any head,
So feel for foolish sinners who must pray,
Shivering, with just one hope, that God's grace may
Save even us from Hell's eternal grind —
That there is Grace enough for everyone.
We're dead and done. Stop jeering. Don't make fun,
But pray to God to pardon all mankind.

Here comes the driving rain to soak and souse
Our bodies; soon the sun will dry us black.
Crows snatch the hairs out from our beards and brows
And peck at sockets where the eyes now lack.
Blown this way that way as the rough wind chances,

Forever we must do our dangling dances,
While rooks who are both hungry and unkind.
Have used our eyes for pincushions: peck, peck.
Make sure your own life's not a futile wreck,
But pray to God to pardon all mankind.

Prince Jesus, mighty Lord of earth and air;
Mortals are fragile, and were not designed
To waste in hell; we have no business there.
Fellow men – don't mock like those whose souls are blind,
But pray to God to pardon all mankind.

Translating poems is an odd business.

Painstakingly accurate prose versions may give a clear sense of the original's meaning, but at the expense of what makes it a poem. A verse translation, on the other hand, must involve radically re-making the poem, not just in a different language, but according to completely different prosodic conventions. Latin likes hexameters, for instance, but these rarely work in English. The best result one can hope for is a version that is not just a weakened copy of the original, but ideally a strong poem in its own right, riffing on the same material as the original.

Not that I despise prose. Making these versions I consulted as many translations into prose as I could find (and sometimes translations into the sort of free verse that is basically prose made pretentious by line-breaks). But the classic poems I chose deserved more than prose – they deserved the zing and buzz that rhyme and traditional metre can offer, to make language come alive.

This collection is of responses to some of the poems in other languages that happen to have taken my fancy. Some of them abridge their originals, slightly; one or two expand them a little. I have taken liberties here and there. My hope is simply that these versions might give readers at least some sense of what attracted me to the originals.

George Simmers